Julie, Linda,

I hope this ─

As you read it.

Thank you so much for buying my book ─ I hope you enjoy it as much as I enjoyed writing it

Jackie Hash

Rhymes with a Reason

Straight from the Heart

JACKIE C. HOUK

Lulu Publishing Services rev. date: 2/17/2017

MY BOOK DEDICATION

This book, *Rhymes With A Reason*, I would like to dedicate to my husband, George, and our two sons David and Bobby. Having these three men in my life has made it complete. God truly blessed me with this family that I love and cherish beyond anything in this world. Each of them has been and continues to be an inspiration for many of my poems. This book of poetry has been a dream of mine for several years and now to George, David and Bobby, I just want to say a Special Thank You. Because of your love, support and encouragement, my dream has now become a reality.

I also want to thank the rest of my family and friends who over the years have been there for me and who believed in me before I ever even believed in myself. Their continuous words of encouragement have kept me on track in pursuing my dream to have my book published.

And to Harry and Todd Craddock my undying love and gratitude for being there for me when I needed you the most.

I Love you all so very much!

As James M. Barrie once said, "Those who bring sunshine into the lives of others cannot keep it from themselves".

Contents

A Book By Its Cover

She had a beauty all her own
and with such style and grace.
Everything about her was perfect.
Not even a hair out of place.

Everyone thought she was unapproachable
but they couldn't have been more wrong.
They thought she was high society
but that is not where she belonged.

She was just an ordinary person
with barely enough money to get by.
She could have had anything she wanted
without even having to try.

But a lonely life she lived
because of the beauty she had.
To look at her you would never think
that she could be so sad.

A lesson to be learned
is what this story is about.
You cannot tell a book by its cover
till you have read it inside and out.

A Favorite Time

My Mom loved to fish
and my step Dad took her a lot.
I have so many memories of going with her
and finding just that special spot.

One morning we got up very early
cause we had a long way to go.
About an hour and half later
we arrived with our boat in tow.

Oh we were so ready to catch fish
but little did we know
my step Dad forgot the boat key
so back to the house we had to go.

So our early morning fishing trip
started out a little bad
but soon turned into
one of the best days I ever had.

The river was so calm
and the sun was just right.
There was a slight breeze blowing
and the fish were waiting to bite.

I never was good at taking off fish
and my Mom knew it too.
She would never say a word
when I handed it to her to do.

The catfish were so big
It was hard getting them to the top.
You would reel and reel
until you just wanted to stop.

Oh but it was so worth it
once you got to see.
The catfish you had on your pole
were as big as big could be.

The sun was starting to set
so we knew it was time to go.
But we would be back again
next time with our boat and key in tow.

A Girl Out On The Street

She was sitting on a corner
outside in the cold.
She was homeless
at least that's what I was told.

I looked at her
without her seeing me.
I wondered to myself
how this came to be?

She didn't look
like all the rest.
She was dirty but clean
and dressed up in her best.

People were passing her by
without even looking her way.
It was so hard for me to realize
that she did this every day.

I went over and stood next to her
and ask if I could sit and talk.
She looked at me and wiped her tears
and ask if we could just take a walk.

I asked about her family
but of course she said she had none.
Before our walk was through
I knew all about them – everyone.

She was thrown out
by some things that she had done.
She said that all she wanted
was to have a little fun.

Her family won't take her back
until she is back on her feet.
So that is why she is
a girl living out on the street.

We stopped at a cafe
and we talked while she ate.
When I looked down
she had completely cleaned her plate.

She had nowhere to go
and no place to sleep.
Home with me she went
to get back on her feet.

She got a job
after a couple of days.
Now I see how God
works in mysterious ways.

She's now working to help the homeless.
Trying with all her might
to get them off the street
and out of the cold at night.

Yes she is back home now
and so very glad to be.
And I'm praying another homeless
I will not have to see.

God has a plan for all of us.
To be in the right place at the right time,
He uses each of us
And this time just happened to be mine.

A Knock At The Door

I hear a knocking.
Should I go to the door?
If I stay very still
will they knock anymore?

Who could it be
this late at night?
Why is their knocking
giving me such a fright?

I call out, Who's There?
But no one will answer me.
Should I open the door
or just let it be?

I listen very carefully
and I hear the knock again.
They are very persistent.
They really want in.

As I ponder on what to do
trying to make up my mind.
I realize it has been 10 minutes
and I'm running out of time.

Open it or not?
Which should it be?
What would you do
If you were me?

A Little Touch

Sometimes at night when I get cold,
I will scoot up next to you in the bed.
You will put your arm around me
and then kiss me lightly upon my head.

You always know how
to make things just right.
You're always there for me
even in the middle of the night.

Just lying there in bed
with your arm around me,
I know that nothing bad will happen
and I'm as safe as can be.

Just the little things that you do
to me mean so much.
Sometimes all it takes
is just a little touch.

A Morning Melody

It's quiet now
but it won't be too long,
before the sounds of the morning
will begin their song.

The melody usually starts
before the sun rise.
But you must listen to hear
you can't see with your eyes.

People heading off to work
with their cars going down the street.
That starts the morning melody
with its own special beat.

The clunking of the trash man
as his truck rolls along,
adds a different sound
to the morning song.

The birds want to join in,
so they start to sing,
and somewhere close by
I hear a cell phone ring.

The early morning walkers
are up walking all about,
which makes the dogs start to bark
and in turn makes the owners shout.

The wind starts to blow
making the wind chimes ring.
What a beautiful sound
to this melody that they bring.

Kids waiting on a school bus
laughing and joking all around,
this too adds to the morning song
with its different sound.

A storm is starting to brew.
The rain comes pouring down.
What a melody all this makes
and you can hear it all around.

The roar of the thunder
adds a mighty touch,
which blends in nicely
and it's not too much.

Things start to get quiet now.
The morning melody is almost thru.
This was just God's way of saying
good morning to all of you.

A Mother's Love

This poem I wrote when my youngest son, Bobby, joined the Marines at the age of 18 and was sent to Iraq in 2004 at the age of 19. It was one of the hardest things I had to do - watch him leave on that bus. This poem is for my son, Bobby who thank God came home safe and sound.

She goes upstairs to his room
and sits on his bed.
She touches his pillow
where he has laid his head.

She looks about the room
and pictures him there.
She sees his brush and comb
that he used on his hair.

She sits at his computer
and leans back in his chair.
Faintly she can still smell the scent
of his cologne lingering in the air.

Everything is so quiet
not a sound does she hear.
She tenderly wipes away
one of her many tears.

She comes up here often
when she needs to cry.
No one else could understand this
no matter how hard they try.

This is her way
to still stay close,
on those days
when she misses him the most.

She misses his loud music
and him running in and out.
"Be right back and I Love you Mom,"
he would turn around and shout.

He got called to serve his country.
Off to Iraq he had to go.
She can't wait till he returns
because she misses him so.

She tries hard not to think
of the things he might have to do.
She has to remember
he's there fighting for me and you.

She knows in her heart
that he won't come back the same boy.
But no matter what
he'll always be - her pride and joy.

A grown man
will return in his place.
Where several hard years
have been etched upon his face.

His boyhood innocence,
he will never get back.
It was replaced by strength and courage
of which he will never lack.

How brave he is
to go so far away.
To fight for his country
and the American way.

We will probably never know
what all he has been thru,
while he was in Iraq
protecting the Red, White and Blue.

She closes her eyes and bows her head
and silently begins to pray.
She thanks God daily
for watching over him every day.

She goes back downstairs
because her life must go on.
She and his Dad will have to wait
until their Marine safely returns back home.

I love you Bobby,
Mom

A New Day

A new day has begun
and yesterday is no more.
I lie in bed and wonder
what today has in store.

How I face it
is totally up to me.
It could be good or bad
so which one do I want it to be?

Do I get up
or stay in bed?
Do I throw back the covers
or cover up my head?

And then I look out my window
and behold what do I see,
one of God's own creations
shining down on me.

I know God is speaking to me
in His own special way.
To you I have given
this beautiful day.

On my knees I get down
and say my morning prayer.
I thank God again
for always being there.

I will make this day
one of my very best.
And I know with God's help
that I can get thru all the rest.

A Thanksgiving Blessing

As Thanksgiving grows near
my blessings become more evident to me.
I'm so thankful to God
and the things he has allowed me to see.

I'm thankful for the sun
and the way it feels upon my face.
And the smell of the rain
after it is finished and leaves its trace.

I'm thankful for the four seasons
and I appreciate each and every one.
However, I am more thankful
when the wintertime is done.

I'm thankful for my childhood
and the memories – good and bad.
I laugh when I think of the good ones
and cry at the ones that made me sad.

I'm thankful for the love
that my parents gave to me.
And for my brothers and sisters
and for all my family.

I'm thankful for the man
that God brought into my life.
I'm so happy that he married me
and made me his wife.

I'm thankful for our boys
and the men they turned out to be.
We are so proud of both of them
their father and me.

I'm thankful for my job
and the family I have here.
Each of you are so special
and to my heart so dear.

I'm thankful for life
and the many blessings I have received.
And I thank God daily
for giving them to me.

As you celebrate this Thanksgiving
count your blessings and thank God for each one.
And the many wonderful things
in your life that he has done.

We have so much
that all of us should be thankful for.
May you all receive a blessing this Thanksgiving
and so much more.

All Alone

I remember when our love was brand new
and we could not wait to be together.
But now you are telling me it is over,
and you are leaving me forever

I never knew you were unhappy.
I wish that I had known.
You said your love for me had died
and now I am left all alone.

We were so happy together.
I thought our love would last.
But now that you are gone
I find myself living in the past

I miss you my love.
But happy is what I want you to be.
And if you ever change your mind,
right here waiting is where you will find me.

Alone In The Dark

I sit alone in the dark
afraid to even breathe.
Why am I so scared
what could have frightened me?

Was it a knock
or just a sound?
Why did I jump out of bed
with such a bound?

If I listen closely
will I hear it once more?
What could have scared me so badly
could it have been someone at the door?

I creep very slowly
and roam all about.
I'm moving very quietly
when I really just want to shout.

No more do I hear it
but what could it have been?
If I go back to bed
will I hear it once again?

Whatever it was
it is now gone.
And I'm once again
left all alone.

Am I?

I sit here sometimes
and wonder about my life.
Have I been a good mother?
Have I been a good wife?

Have things turned out
the way that I dreamed?
Am I living in an imaginary world?
Are things really what they seem?

I have tried to do
the very best that I could.
Sometimes life doesn't always
turn out the way we think it should.

You do your best
but you always hope for more.
But you never know
what life holds in store.

If you could see into the future
and see how things will be,
would you do anything differently
after what you may see?

Life is not for us to change
but live it from day to day.
Make the most of it
come what may.

We are not perfect people.
We just do the best we can.
We have to learn to turn things over
and give it to "The Man".

I just hope
in some small way,
that my children have learned to do
the best they can each day.

To my husband one thing I want to say
to you I have always been true,
and all my love
I have given only to you.

So the answer to my question,
if I have been a good wife and mother.
I've done the very best that I could
and loved them like no other.

We are not here on this earth
to do everything right.
Even though we try
with all of our might.

We are human
and we do make mistakes.
And from them
the consequences we take.

So always do the best you can
and never give in,
to thinking you are not worthy
because you will never win!

Back When

I love to remember my childhood
and things that happened then.
Life was so much simpler.
Oh to go back there again.

The place where I grew up
was just a small community.
It was known as the Village
and your neighbors were like family.

No video games did we have,
so outside we would stay.
Hopscotch, baseball and kick the can
were some of the games we would play.

Our Dad would whistle
when it was time to go home.
We didn't have street lights
but you weren't afraid to walk alone.

People got along back then.
There were no fussing or fights.
We didn't even lock our doors
when we went to bed at night.

We didn't have much money
but we always had plenty to eat.
My Mom was such a good cook.
Her meals you just couldn't beat.

No drugs, gangs or guns
and the worries were few.
I wish that today was more like then
How about you?

Banging At Your Door

Sometimes when life's problems
are banging at your door.
You wonder what you are going to do
because you just can't take it anymore.

Take a look deep inside yourself
and see the person that you are.
You can fight whatever comes your way
and beat it by far.

You just have to have faith
in the man up above.
And he will show you
just what you are made of.

He doesn't give us
more than what we can take.
Even though it seems
all we make are mistakes.

Just know he will be there for you
no matter what comes your way.
If you believe in him,
You can get thru each and every day.

So start your day off right
by saying a morning prayer.
And know that no matter what
God will always be there.

Your problems won't seem as bad.
As they did once before.
And no more banging
Will you hear at your door.

Before 1985

I didn't give my heart away
so easily to you.
The hurt that I felt once before
still felt so new.

You would come by my office
and one thing you would always say,
I'm going to marry you before 1985
and then you would just walk away.

We started out as friends
but then it turned to so much more.
I couldn't wait to see you each day
when you would come by my door.

My love for you started to grow
and it wasn't very long,
before I finally realized
by your side was where I belonged.

We got married on Valentine's day
and the year was 1982.
What you use to say about 1985
really did come true.

One of the happiest moments
that ever happened in my life,
was when I walked down the aisle
and became your wife.

Until the day that I die
I just want you to know,
that my love for you
will only continue to grow.

And when from this earth
I finally do depart,
the love that I feel for you
will always remain deep inside my heart.

Bobby's Papers

Our boys are grown now
but when they were small,
they gave us so many good memories
and this is one of the best of all.

At the dinner table each night
we would tell about our day.
It was my younger son, Bobby's time
and this is what he had to say.

Mom, I knew you really wouldn't like it
if bad grades I brought home.
So when the teacher wasn't looking
I threw those papers in the trash where they belong.

Bobby I said – You cannot throw papers away
just because you thought you could.
You have to bring those home to me
just like the teacher said you should.

He said that the teacher saw what he did
and out of his trash, got the papers he threw away.
she gave them back to Bobby to bring home
for the second time that day.

I thought this was the ending to his story
and the papers he brought home to me.
So I told him when dinner was over
to get the papers out for me to see.

Oh no this was not the ending
and those papers never made it home.
He said when the teacher wasn't looking
back in the trash they went where they belong.

Car Wash

I went to a car wash
not too long ago.
One of those automated things
that pulls you thru kind of slow.

The guy motioned for me
to pull my car on in.
He said to put it in neutral
and that's when my troubles begin.

All of a sudden my car started shaking
like it was trying to go back.
I thought somehow I had gotten
completely off the track.

The car kept shaking
and jerking all about.
I rolled down my window
and started to shout.

You're tearing up my car
I told the two men.
One shouted you got it in reverse
while the other one just grinned.

I could see he was laughing
thinking this was going to be fun.
All I could think of
was the damage that it may have done.

The one guy was very insistent,
Lady, you have it in reverse.
He was getting a little upset.
I thought he was going to curse.

The other guy thought it was funny
and I could hear him say
this is the best laugh
I've had all day.

I just knew I had put it in neutral
but when I looked down to see.
I saw that it really was in reverse
I was embarrassed as could be.

When I saw my mistake
I knew what I had to do.
I finally put it in neutral
and it pulled me on thru.

I will never forget that day
And I'm sure neither will those men.
But I knew that I would never
go to that car wash again.

Changing For The Better

He made a mistake
as we all sometimes do.
But he got caught.
Now he has to pay his due.

He really was a good kid
but went wrong along the way.
He saw his mistakes too late
when they arrested him that day.

It was dark by the time they booked him
and they took him to his cell.
When he walked in he saw the sign
That said – Welcome To Hell!

This is what it took
to finally make him see.
His life had to change.
This is not what he wanted it to be.

He knew what he had to do
and he wanted to make things right.
He got down on his knees and prayed
and gave his life to God that night.

Lord I'm sorry for what I did.
So I'm asking forgiveness from you.
If you will help and guide me
I know that I can get thru.

He served his time and got out.
And today he is a completely different man.
He gives talks to young people
And tells them all about "God's plan"

Changing World

Is the world moving too fast
or is it just me,
remembering the old ways
of how things used to be.

It just seems to me
that we need to slow down some.
Take time to enjoy life
and have a little fun.

It's all just rush rush
and how much money we can make.
We've gotten away from our values
how much more can we take?

Maybe it's me that needs to speed up
and be more like people today.
I don't know about that though
I kinda like the old fashion way.

Change is supposed to be good
But do we have to go along?
What if we stayed the way we are
Is that right or wrong?

The values that we have today
are nothing like we had before.
It's the little things that I miss
like people just holding open a door.

What happened to yes ma'am and no sir
and of course please and thank you.
Do people even say these anymore?
I just don't have a clue.

Change is good
to this I do agree,
but only to a certain point
it shouldn't change the inner me.

We have to keep up with technology
this I know to be true.
But don't give up our values.
Do you feel this way too?

We need to stand up more
and fight for our rights.
Or one day we will look back
and what we see will give us such a fright.

It's not too late
and then again it may be.
I do know if changes are to be made
it will be up to you and me.

Christmas Past

The Christmas tree is all decorated
and the lights are flashing off and on.
I sit back to relax and in my mind
I'm going to a place that once was home.

It's the night before Christmas
and Dad took us out to see the lights.
When we would get back home
it would be late and time to say good night.

We were so excited that sleep would not come
so out of our bed we would leap.
Down the hallway and to the living room
we would barely creep.

The Christmas lights illuminated the living room
just enough so that we could see,
the gifts that Santa had brought
and left underneath our Christmas tree

We didn't get much back then
the way the kids do today.
We were lucky to get one toy
but we were used to it that way.

Paulette, Michael and I
were as quiet as a mouse.
As we looked at the toys
that Santa had left at our house.

I remember that night so vividly
and the trouble that we got into.
But it was all Paulette's fault
because she didn't do what she was supposed to.

Michael had gotten a little car
and I got a doll and started to play.
Little did we know
our world was about to go astray.

That year Paulette got a radio
and she just couldn't wait you see.
She turned it on and the volume was up
she sure got us in trouble, us three.

My Dad yelled out
you kids get back in bed.
And we knew we had better
because he meant what he said

Michael and I were both mad at Paulette
because she got us in trouble you know.
But we did go back to bed
and off to sleep we finally did go.

I look again at my tree
and the lights that are flashing off and on.
And oh how I miss those days
and that place that I once called Home!

Coming Home

We never knew he was on board
for not a sound did he make.
No one knew about the precious cargo
that from the hull they would take.

When we reached our destination
and after we did land.
The captain came out of his cabin
and told us about this fine young man.

We have someone on board
that we would like to depart first.
And we looked out the windows
that's when we saw the hearse.

For as far as you could see
service men and women were there,
one of their own was finally back home
and they bowed their heads in prayer.

As the door of the hull opened
and the coffin they did see.
The American flag was draped over it
just as it should be.

This brave young man had given his life.
He had fought and done his best.
And now he was brought back home
where he would finally be laid to rest.

Deception

Deception is such a dirty word
but yet it has become a part of me.
When you keep secrets deep within
that is how you turn out to be.

Something that was so small
you thought that you could hide.
But the more you kept it in
the more it ate you up inside.

You can't even look in the mirror
you're afraid of what you might see.
That person that is staring back
is no longer me.

When you reached the point
that you can no longer hold,
that awful secret that is within
you finally let it be told.

When he finally hears the truth
you take a look at his face,
the love that was once there
is gone without a trace.

Was it worth it?
Holding that secret in for so long?
You have lost everything.
In his life you no longer belong.

You ask for his forgiveness
but he just looks away,
all you can do is wait and see
if he will forgive you one day.

Don't Fade Away

You can't make yourself be happy
when you are feeling so sad.
You can't go back into the past
and relive what you had.

You have to pick yourself up
and do the best that you can.
You have to show everyone
you can do it - you're the man.

You can't let yourself
just fade away.
You have to keep going
and face each new day.

You will find the answers
to help you get thru.
But you have to get up,
it all starts with you.

Fight those feelings
of hurt, anguish, and pain.
And replace them with
love and kindness and see what you gain.

You have a reason to live
and a purpose to go on.
We will be there for you
on the days you can't make it on your own.

So my friend that is what you will always be
and these words I give to you.
On those hard days that you will have
I hope in some way they will get you thru.

Dreams

We are never too old
to dream our dreams.
We are never too old
but yet it seems.

Our bodies say we can't
but our minds disagree.
My heart says do
whatever lets me - be Me!

Yes I may be a little older.
But too old I will never be,
to live out my dreams
and make new memories.

Duty Calls

She got up very early that morning
no sleep had she the night before.
This day was going to be very hard for her
and she knew there would be many more.

Her youngest son was leaving home today.
He got his notice to go to Iraq.
She was so afraid to let herself think
that he might not be coming back.

She and his Dad would take him to his unit
where all the other soldiers would be.
Although his uniform made him look grown up
her baby boy was all she could see.

He wasn't even 19 years old yet
so why was he the one that had to go?
But she knew this day was coming
when he joined the Marines a few months ago.

She looked at him while he stood in line
waiting for them to issue his gun.
She didn't want to think of the things he had to do
because this was her son.

When the buses pulled up
her tears just started to flow.
She knew she promised not to cry
but she couldn't stand to see him go.

She ran to him
and held onto him as tight as she could.
You take care of yourself and come back home
like you promised me that you would.

He smiled and told her not to worry
that he had a job to go and do.
And before he boarded the bus
He turned and said, " Mom, I love you"

She stood there helplessly
until the buses she could no longer see.
She closed her eyes and prayed to God
please take care of him for me.

Escaping Reality

Sometimes I will close my eyes
to escape reality,
and take my mind
where things cannot get to me.

I reflect on happy times
when everything seemed right.
To get back there again
I try with all my might.

I don't want to face tomorrow
or what might be ahead.
I rather close my eyes
and be here instead.

This place I go
when the truth I don't want to hear,
is a place where I hold close
everything that is so dear.

I know when I'm here
only good things will I see,
no trouble or bad things
can bother me.

I can't hide forever
my eyes I will have to open
and listen to the words
to me that were spoken.

Learn to let it go
and turn it over to Him.
He will always be there
even when things look dim.

My friends are right
I know this is true.
He will always be there
for me and for you.

To Him I will give my troubles
so I can face this day.
I know with His guidance
He will show me the way.

Everyday Things

What if for one day,
we had no power,
no electricity or water,
not even for an hour.

We had to go back to the basics
that would be so hard to do.
Because you see we are spoiled
yes we both are – me and you.

There would be no alarm clock
to get us up.
There would be no coffee
waiting to be poured into a cup.

No hot shower
would we be able to take.
No hot breakfast
would we be able to make.

No light to see by
only candles to light.
No heat or air
to warm or to cool us at night.

These are but a few things
we expect to have each day.
If you had to do without them
could you find another way?

We take so much for granted
that it's time we stop to say,
Lord we are so blessed and we thank you
For the things you give to us each day.

Forgive Me Lord

Lord if you have a few minutes
I need to spend some time with you.
I have some decisions to make
and I need your help on what to do.

You see Lord I haven't been the best person
and the mistakes I've made are more than one.
It's causing such a battle within myself
and I can't undo the damage that it has done.

I cannot look at myself in the mirror
for that person I don't like to see.
I'm so sorry Lord that I'm such a mess
I don't know what has happened to me.

I can't even begin to forgive myself
so Lord how can I expect you too.
Can you please help me Lord
and show me what I must do?

I'm listening to you Lord
and I will do what you say.
I want to be a better person
and I will start right away.

Tomorrow is a whole new day
and I will start it off right.
I will say my prayers to you
both morning and again at night.

With your help Lord
I know things will change for me.
With you in my heart
I will be the best that I can be.

I know how precious your time is Lord
and I appreciate you spending it with me.
I'm going to be a better person
on this I guarantee.

Found My Home

I wander from place to place
because I live out on the streets.
At night I'm always looking
for a warm place where I can sleep.

Today as I was walking around,
this beautiful building I did see.
Even though I had never been inside
it seemed to be beckoning me.

I knew right away it was a church.
I felt so welcomed right from the start.
A warm feeling of finally belonging
was completely filling my heart.

The church was so warm and inviting.
My fears were no longer there.
I went down front to the altar
and bowed my head in prayer.

I knew I had found my new home.
God was watching out for me.
I would no longer wander the streets
I found the place where I was meant to be.

Getting Older?

Birthdays come each year
and we get older when they do.
But how you look at aging
depends entirely upon you.

You can look and think you're old
when really you're not.
Our bodies are not like they used to be
we're not young and hot.

We're dragging and sagging
in all the wrong places.
And oh all the wrinkles
that have appeared upon our faces.

We might think twice
before we get down.
Because sometimes we have to have help
getting back up off the ground.

Our home looks like a pharmacy
because of all the pills we have to take.
But to get thru the day's aches and pains
this is the sacrifice we have to make.

Growing old graciously
is what I always wanted to do.
To get out and enjoy life and get around
just like I use to.

But my body is telling me
there are certain things you can no longer do.
But I'm not going to stand for that
how about you?

We may be older in years
and in our body a little too.
But keep young in your heart
and live life like you want to.

My wish for you Harry is this.
May all your birthday wishes come true
And may you be able to blow out all the candles
without spitting on your birthday cake too!

Goodbye Paulette

You left so quickly
I didn't get to say goodbye.
Now all I can do
is just sit here and cry.

I couldn't comprehend
when they called to say.
They had some bad news
you had just passed away.

I can't make myself believe
that you are no longer here.
I just want to hear your voice
and know that you are still near.

I'm just being selfish
because I love you so.
I just wasn't ready
I didn't want you to go.

So many emotions
I'm feeling right now.
I'm trying to sort thru them
someway – somehow.

A smile just came across my face
from a memory that I have of you.
On one of our Christmas trips
and some of the things we used to do.

How much fun we use to have
and we would laugh and joke all day.
And then we would go to eat
and celebrate your birthday.

Well today there is another celebration
with singing and shouting everywhere.
Mother came down to get you
and she took you up there.

One day we will all be together
as a family once more.
And you will be there to greet us
as we come through Heaven's door

Happy 33rd Anniversary

Valentine's Day is very special
particularly to me and you.
It was 33 years ago today
when we said I do.

It was a beautiful Sunday afternoon
the day that I walked down the aisle.
When you looked up and saw me,
you had the sweetest smile.

Gosh you were so handsome
just standing there waiting for me.
When you took my hand in yours,
I knew by your side I was meant to be.

Never did I dream
I would have a love so true.
But everything that I had ever dreamed of
I found when I married you

I looked into your eyes
and so much love did I see.
It took my breath away
when I realized that love was for me.

I don't know where the years have gone
time has slipped away so fast.
But I know that our love has grown deeper
with each day that has passed.

I love you today, tomorrow and forever
and I know this much is true.
That as much as I love you
I know you love me that much too!

Happy Anniversary

**I wrote this for my sister and brother-in-law's
anniversary a couple of years ago.**

**When you find the person you love,
you know you have found your soul mate.
So you start making plans for the future
and set your wedding date.**

**The big day finally comes
and you walk down the aisle.
Your heart literally skips a beat
when you see him smile.**

You look so beautiful
and he is so handsome too.
This marriage was meant to be
between the two of you.

You said your vows
and promised to be true.
When the question was asked
you answered I do.

On that day
man and wife you did become.
It's no longer I and you
you're now only One.

A commitment you made
to each other.
To love, honor and obey
and forsake all others.

Several years have now gone by
and the children have all grown.
Be thankful you still have each other
and you are not alone.

You both are older now
and your marriage is no longer new.
But you still have him
and he still has you.

You've been together
now for many years
You have shared the happy times
and wiped away a few tears

As your anniversary approaches,
remember back to your wedding day.
And the love you have for each other
will get you thru come what may.

So on this anniversary
Paulette & Harry, here's my wish for you.
May the two of you always be as happy
as when you said I do.

Happy?

What makes you happy
have you ever wondered this?
Is it something tangible
or just a loved one's kiss?

There is so much beauty around us
But do we really see?
Are we just too busy to look
You and me?

Life is too short
not to stop now and then.
Don't ever regret
what could have been.

Take time to smell the roses
and enjoy the view.
We should do more of this
me and you.

We rush and rush
to get somewhere.
But is it worth it
Once we get there

Try stopping one day
Just for a minute or two.
And look at all the wonderful things
That God has given to you.

Haunting Memories

I went to a place today
that I don't often go.
Way deep into my mind
because it scares me so.

There are things I put there
that I wanted to forget.
But there are still times
they come back to me yet.

They were bad memories
of something that scared me.
So I put it way back in my mind
thinking they would no longer be.

My thoughts were such
that if I pushed them far enough,
I could no longer remember
that terrible stuff.

That they would disappear
and leave me alone,
and make me think
that they had finally gone.

But all I really did
was to forget it for a day.
When what I wanted to do
was make them go totally away.

Heaven

Have you ever wondered about Heaven
and how it will be?
Will the loved ones who have gone before us
remember you and me?

Are the streets really lined with gold?
Do the angels really have wings?
Do you ever really stop and think
about all these wonderful things?

It must be a magnificent place
and one day we too shall see.
This place called Heaven
where God has saved a place for you and me.

Just think of all the wonders
that will be yours to behold.
These things you will remember forever
because in Heaven you never grow old.

Heaven has no imperfections
there the blind will see and the lame will walk
and those who could not speak before
will now be able to talk.

In our world there are so many beliefs
but one thing I know is true.
There is a heaven and a God
and He is always there for me and you.

He will never turn his back on us
His love is far too deep.
Those times that we neglect Him
if you listen, you can hear Him weep.

If you truly believe in God
then your sins He will forgive,
And in His love and grace
You will always live.

We all must live and die
that much is true,
And what you believe thereafter
Is entirely up to you.

As for me, I know God is real
and that heaven truly is a wonderful place.
One day I will see all of this
when I finally see Jesus face to face.

Yes Heaven is a place
and one day there I will be.
And all of God's glory
I will finally get to see.

My loved ones will be there to greet me
with their arms opened wide,
and Jesus will be there too
right by their side.

That day will be here soon
of that I have no doubt.
and when that glorious day comes
With my loved ones, I will sing and shout.

His Winning Moment

He could feel the sweat
building up inside.
All he really wanted to do
was just find a place to hide.

He stepped out of the dugout
he was next at bat.
He kept wiping the sweat
that was now dripping from his hat.

It was the last game of the series
and it was a tied ball game.
Whomever won this game
their team would never be the same.

Two outs already
and bases loaded too.
He stepped up to the plate.
he knew what he had to do.

The first pitch was a ball.
maybe he could walk in a run.
Strike the umpire called
where did that pitch come from?

He had to pay attention
so he stepped away from the plate.
He had to clear his head and get into the game
before it was too late.

The crowd was yelling
they wanted us to win.
He took a swing at the next pitch
It went into a spin.

Foul ball yelled the umpire
Now the count was two and one.
Come on get it together
And get this hit done.

Another ball went by the plate
now it was two and two.
He still had a chance to get a walk
but it was going to be hard to do.

Ball three the umpire cried
the crowd went wild.
It was full count and two outs
the next pitch he just smiled.

He hit it hard and the ball went sailing
and he started to run.
All the other players had scored
and he was left the only one.

He ran like there was no tomorrow
not knowing if they caught the ball or not.
He just knew he had to make it home
this was his time to shine in the spot.

As he rounded third
he saw his teammates at home plate.
It wasn't just a home run he hit
it was a grand slam and that was Great!

They gave him the game ball
for making the winning run.
He was so glad that it was over
and that the ballgame he had won!

I Do

She couldn't believe this day was here.
The day she dreamed about all her life.
She was about to walk down the aisle
to finally become his wife.

She remembered when she was little
how she wanted everything to be.
Now she was about to take that big step
and make her dreams a reality.

She couldn't wait to see his face
to see what he would do.
Would he really shed a tear
she wished that she knew.

She looked like an angel
in her dress made of satin and lace.
Everything about her was perfect
not even a hair out of place.

Her life was about to change
it would never be the same.
When this day was over
she would even have a new name.

She could hear the music
it was almost time.
Her cue to walk down the aisle
was when the bells started to chime.

Her Dad held out his arm
the time had actually come.
Soon there would no longer be two of them
they would be joined together as one.

She repeated the words
till death do us part.
I promise to love you
with all of my heart.

The ceremony was over
and after they said I do.
She turned to him and said
I truly do love you.

They were now man and wife
her big day was almost thru.
She would remember this day forever
when all her dreams came true.

If Only

Oh if only we had the hindsight
to see what our mistakes can do.
Then there would be no more regrets
for either me or you.

But we do make mistakes
and the consequences are there.
And whether we like it or not
life isn't always fair.

I once loved someone
with every beat of my heart.
But it seemed our love was doomed
right from the very start.

I still remember the night he left
and how I cried all night long.
I thought my life had ended
when he went out the door and was gone.

But we both met someone new
and went our separate ways.
but God how I wish he only knew
that I still care for him today.

I'm Not Me

I'm not myself tonight
and I can't understand why.
All I really want to do
is be by myself and cry.

What has changed about me?
This is not how I want to be.
I feel so depressed
when earlier I was so happy.

I'm not being social.
My family sees a change in me.
They're all playing games
I just want them to leave me be.

I don't like this person
that I seemed to have become.
Why am I like this
what was it that I have done?

So many emotions
I'm feeling inside
I just want to run away
and go somewhere and hide.

I've got to make these feelings
completely go away.
Maybe tomorrow they will be gone
and I can start a whole new day.

I hope that my family understands
it is just something that I'm going thru.
And they will forgive me
for the things I did or didn't do.

So when tomorrow comes
I guess I will just have to wait and see
if this different person is still here
or that I have gone back to being me.

I'm Thankful

Lord if you have a few minutes
could I take a little of your time?
I just want to tell you
some things I have on my mind.

I just want you to know
how thankful I am today.
For all the blessings in my life
that you have sent my way.

I'm thankful for my husband
and the love he brought into my life.
I love him more today
than when I became his wife.

I thank you for our two sons
and what it has meant to me
to be the wife and mother
of this most wonderful family.

I thank you for my sister and brother
and for their families too.
And I can't forget my loved ones
who are up in heaven with you.

Thank you for my friends
and the bond that made us so.
I love them all very dearly
and just wanted to let them know.

So I thank you Lord
for this time out of your precious day
And even more so
for listening to what I had to say.

It Couldn't Be

His blue eyes were mesmerizing.
He just melted my heart.
The minute I saw him
I just fell apart.

I knew I could love him
for the rest of my life.
But it just wasn't meant to be
he already had a wife.

My love for him grew more everyday
and I knew that he loved me too.
We tried so hard to make it work
but he knew what he had to do.

One night he came over
and told me he found someone new.
My world ended that night
I did not know what I was going to do.

I knew he did it for me
so that I could find someone too.
And eventually I did
and his love was so true.

There is still a part of me
that wonders to this day.
What my life would have been like
if things had went another way.

Even though 40 years have come and gone.
I still think about him today.
And I wonder if he too
thinks about me in the same way.

There will always be a special place in my heart
where his memories will always be.
And who knows maybe his heart too
has a place where he holds memories of me.

Just Being A Mom

She gets up each morning
way before the others.
She gets things ready for the day
Why, because she is a Mother!

She starts breakfast
fixing all the things they like to eat.
She irons their clothes
so they will all look so neat

She packs their lunch
and has them ready to go.
She puts a little note inside
that says I love you so.

She doesn't do it because it is expected
or that they told her to.
She does it because she loves them
and that is what she wants to do.

She's very thankful for her family
and this is just her way to say
how much she truly loves them
each and every day

Leap of Faith

When I walked down the aisle
to stand next to you,
it was with a leap of faith
when I said I do.

We are not guaranteed
anything in our life.
But I knew on that day
I would always be your wife.

When you took my hand
and placed on the ring,
you said this was just the start
of only good things.

With you I found
what I always searched for,
Love and faith
and so much more.

After all these years
we are still going strong.
With our love, faith and trust
we can never go wrong.

Left or Right?

I ran into a crossroad
on my journey the other day.
It made me stop and ponder
which would be the right way?

Do I go left or right?
I know not which path to take.
I know I can't stay here forever
a decision I must make.

Life gives us crossroads
that we must face every day.
If you make the decision with your heart
you will always choose the right way!

Sometimes we don't listen
to our hearts when they speak.
So we choose the wrong path
then we must face the havoc that they wreak.

You will come to those crossroads in life
and you must choose the path to go.
Open up your heart and listen
and the right path you will know.

But if you choose wrongfully
the consequences you must endure.
Listen to your heart when you choose
So you will know for sure!

Lies

When we hurt the ones we love
the pain we too feel.
You can't take it back
it is so very real.

You can see it in their eyes
when they look at you.
They will never forget
no matter what you do.

It doesn't matter how it happened
or when or where.
You just know you have hurt them
beyond repair.

If your love is strong enough
you can continue your life.
But will it be enough
to continue to be man and wife.

Secrets are lies
when you keep them from another.
Trust will have to be earned again
with each other.

Take it from me
be honest and true,
Please do as I say
And not as I do!

Living Off Of Love

I get up each morning
and off to work I go.
As for my husband
he retired almost 10 years ago.

Sometimes he is still in bed
just sleeping away.
While I go to work
and earn a living each day.

Someone asked him
not long ago,
how he was making it being retired.
His answer is something you should know.

He says that we can live off love
as long as love goes to work each day.
I guess this refers to me
and I just have one thing to say.

One day I too shall retire
then what will he say or do.
I can just hear him now
saying these words to you.

We will live off social security
and make the best of it.
But we could have more
if my wife hadn't quit.

So until my retirement day
finally comes true.
We will continue living off love
just like he was used to.

Looking Back At Me

When I look into the mirror
and truly look at what I see.
I see an older woman
staring back at me.

I don't see a beauty
that I never was you see.
I see a wife and a mother
Because that is all I ever wanted to be.

As I look at this woman
that I have become
I look back at my life
and at the job I have done.

I didn't do everything right
even though I tried.
There were days when I laughed,
and days when I cried.

But my sons turned out alright
so a good job I guess I did do.
My husband and I are still together
and still so in love too.

When I look back again in the mirror
this time this is what I did see.
The face of a happily married woman and mother
and that is a true reflection of Me.

Looking Back

I'm cleaning out my memories
and thought I would start with you.
It's been a long time since it ended
and I just need to accept we are thru.

Before I delete them completely
I'll look back to see.
And try and figure out what happened
between you and me.

I thought your love for me
would never end.
But the truth really was
you only wanted to be my friend.

I loved you too much
for it to be that way.
So I told you goodbye
and I left and went away.

I heard that you got married
and that you are very happy too.
I'm so glad to know
that you found someone new.

I've also moved on
with a new man in my life.
I love him very much
so I became his wife.

Your memories are now all gone
because I no longer look back to the past.
My heart is filled with my new love
and I know it will forever last.

Love After All These Years

When I look into your eyes
and see the love that is there for me,
my heart could almost burst
with all that love I see.

Just a slight touch of your hand
or the way you look at me,
makes me feel all gooey inside
just the way love is supposed to be.

We have that kind of love
and have had it for many years.
Of course we had our ups and downs
but also much laughter and tears.

We've always been there for each other
and will always continue to be.
I will always be there for you
as I know you are there for me.

Our love is never ending
It will always be You and I,
we will always be together
until the day that we die.

I never thought someone would love me
as much as I love them.
But I found that love in you
for you truly are a rare gem.

On that very special day
the day that we said I do,
I knew your love for me would be forever
Just as mine would too.

When we get older
and look back upon our life,
I will turn to you and say
I love being your wife.

Man of My Dreams

You know sometimes we need to look
at how we are blessed.
We need to look at what we have
and forget about all the rest.

I'm thankful for the man
that God has given to me.
He is the most wonderful person
that ever could be.

No he is not Robert Redford or Brad Pitt.
But he is handsome in his own way.
Just hearing him say that he loves me
truly makes my whole day.

He's the man of my dreams
because he made them all come true.
On the day we were married
when he said I Do.

I know he truly loves me
with all of his heart.
We will always be together
and only death will make us part.

Michael, My Big Brother

I want to tell you about someone
who's really like no other.
His name is Michael
and he's my Big Brother.

Everyone needs a brother
especially one like him.
He's really something special
he's like a rare gem.

He looked after me when I was little
And he is still there for me today
I know how much he loves me
And I feel exactly the same way

I have memories of him
When we were small
I remember looking up to him so much
Like he was ten feet tall

Mother used to tell me
How protective he used to be
He would always keep biscuits in his pockets
One for him and one for me

He's a down to earth type guy
a really one of a kind.
No better man if you looked
will you ever find.

He's never wanted for much
his needs are very few.
And when you ever need him
he will always be there for you.

He is a great carpenter
he can build so many things.
What he builds lasts forever
and oh the joy that it brings.

He reminds me of our Dad
in his looks and manners too.
He is always a perfect gentleman
and everyone will agree too.

He's been there for me
whether I needed him or not.
I could just turn around
and there he is, johnny on the spot.

He's someone that I admire
and I just wanted him to know.
I'm so glad that he's my brother
because I dearly love him so.

Miracles Do Happen

They say that miracles do happen
however they have never happened to me.
But I'm looking at a miracle now
and this is what I see.

My Mother is standing in front of me
and she's been gone for almost 6 years.
I can't believe she is actually here
but I see her even thru my tears.

I run to her and hug her tight
I'm afraid she will disappear.
When I can finally speak
I ask, "How did you get here?"

It doesn't matter is all she said
we've been given this day.
There is so much that I want to tell you
and so much that I want to say.

I couldn't quit looking at her.
Was she really real?
I closed my eyes and opened them again
and yet there she stood... still.

She was so young and beautiful
I found all I could do was stare.
I looked deep into her eyes
and saw no pain there.

I asked her about Heaven
and this is what she told me.
It is the most wonderful place
you could ever want to be.

Jesus will be there to take your hand
when your time on this earth is thru.
You will never want for anything again
everything is right there for you.

There is no hatred and no war.
Only love and peace do you see.
Heaven has a place there
for all those that do believe.

Before we knew it our time was over
it had gone much too fast.
I wanted to hold onto her forever
and make this moment last.

She told me she had to go
that our time together was thru.
Before she left she turned to say,
just remember I am always there with you.

Mother

As I walk by the window
I happen to see,
someone outside
that is looking in at me.

My heart is racing
can this be true?
This person that I see
Mother is it really you?

I start to tremble
I can't believe this is real.
If I close and open up my eyes again
will you be there still?

I miss you so much
your voice I long to hear.
Can it really be you
that is so close and near?

I stand so still
I'm frozen in place.
I can't believe
I can almost see your face.

Please come nearer
so that I can see.
That it is really you
outside my window looking at me.

I'm trying to think
of what I can do.
So that I can get
closer to you.

If I leave this window
to come out and see,
Will you still be there
waiting for me?

So much I want to say
but all I really want to do,
Is just to tell you how much
we all love and miss you.

I reach down to raise the window
so you can come inside with me.
But when I look up again
your face I no longer see.

You're no longer standing there
and I start to cry.
I cannot find you
no matter how hard I try.

I run outside
and go to the place,
where you were just standing
but you left no trace.

I call your name
and search for you,
but I know you're gone
and there's nothing I can do.

I know you will come back
and when you do,
I will be there at the window
waiting and watching for you.

My Eyes Are Open

I'm all alone in my room
everyone else has gone home.
The hallways are quiet and dark
and I am feeling so alone.

I'm in the hospital recovering from surgery
and I have to stay for an extra day.
The medication they gave me
makes me feel like I'm still in a daze

I wake up for a while
but eventually I go right back to sleep.
Sometimes I think I see the nurse
when she opens the door to take a peek.

I start to dream and it's one I had before
I thought I had heard a sound.
But I can't move or open my eyes
And there's no one else around.

I'm getting nervous and I start to panic
I tell myself that this is only a dream.
Somehow I have to make myself realize
that things just aren't the way they seem.

I hear my door opening again
but still I can't open my eyes.
I'm hearing several different voices
and someone shouting surprise.

Before I know it my dream is over
and I can see my friends looking at me.
I'm so glad that things are back to normal
and that I can move and see.

My Happy Place

The sun is just barely peaking over the horizon
as it starts to spread its warming light.
I look around and find a special place
where I can watch this ending of night.

What a magnificent display of colors
as the sun slowly burst thru.
I sit in awe of this wonderous transition
and marvel at the things He can do.

I close my eyes and it takes me away
to places that are only in my dreams,
I hear the waves as they rush to the shore
oh how pleasant everything seems.

These eminent wonders
that I have been so blessed to see
will forever remain in my heart
because they bring such a peace to me.

I have found my Happy Place
that will be forever etched into my mind.
It will be my place to go
when sometimes I feel so confined.

The sun has now made its grand entrance
and lit the world for everyone to see.
Oh what a wonderful day
this has truly turned out to be.

My Heart Is Hurting

It's early morn
and I sit quietly in the night,
trying to hold back these tears
with all my might.

My heart is heavy
and I feel so sad.
Someone dear has hurt me
and it hurts so bad.

I guess what they say
Is really true,
The ones that you love the most
are the ones that can really hurt you.

The sun is now rising.
A new day is about to begin.
Before I get up to start my day
I say a prayer to God for this hurt to end.

I rise from my chair
and with God's help, this day I will get thru.
And even though my heart is hurting
I will always love you.

My Husband, My Friend, My Lover

I waited all my life
for you to come along,
because by your side
is where I belong.

You are my knight in shining armor.
Everything that I always dreamed of.
We were made for each other
by the man up above.

When I look into your eyes
and all that love that I see.
It is so hard for me to realize
it is there only for me.

I never knew this was how
love was supposed to be.
That I could love someone so much
and they would feel the same about me.

You are not only my husband
you are my lover and my friend,
and I know we will be together
until the very end.

There is not a day that goes by
That you don't say I love you.
And I know it comes from deep inside your heart
because you truly do.

When your arms are around me
and you hold me so close,
these are the times
that I love you the most.

When I have bad dreams
and wake up in such a fright,
I know you are there beside me
and everything is going to be alright.

You are my strength and inspiration
that I need each and every day.
And when I need you
you are always there come what may.

You are the light of my world
and know that this comes from my heart.
I love you dearly
and from your side I will never part.

In our twilight years
together we will still be.
Because I love you
and I know you love me.

My Knight In Shining Armor

Sometimes I wake up
from crying in the night.
I had a bad dream
and it gave me such a fright.

But you are always there
to calm me down.
It is so nice to know
you are always around.

I depend on you
though independent I try to be.
I like the way
you take such good care of me.

You're the strength
that gets me through.
I don't know where I would be
if it weren't for you.

We were friends when
I first met you.
But then became soul mates
the day we said I do.

I knew when I married you
it was until death do us part.
When I said I do
it was with all my heart.

I've grown closer to you
with each passing day.
I know I will always be with you
come what may.

You have my heart
my soul and my love.
I know you were sent to me
from the man up above.

Your love I treasure
more than my own life.
You made me so very happy
the day I became your wife.

My Legacy To You

When from this earth
I do depart,
to you I will leave my legacy
that comes from my heart.

I can leave no money
for there is none to give,
no fame or fortune
on which you can live.

The words that I leave you
is all there will be,
nothing else do I have
for you to remember me.

To no one else
will they be worth anything,
and to you
no fortune will they bring.

They are just words
that I wrote just for you,
and thru life's disappointments
hopefully will somehow get you thru.

I hope you will enjoy them
and read them each day,
and that they will give you comfort
in some small way.

And thru my legacy
you will come to see,
that in my heart
you will always be.

My Life With You

I see you standing there
but you don't see me.
And I think to myself
how lucky can one person be.

You're everything that I always wanted
all rolled into one.
I don't know how I got so lucky
or what it was that I had done.

We have had such a wonderful life
and we still have many years yet to go.
I have so much love in my heart for you
that I just want you to know.

I think back to our first kiss
and how it thrilled me so.
I've loved you for so long
and my love just continues to grow.

You turn around and see me there
and it makes my heart skip a beat.
I know with you by my side
I need nothing more – my life is complete.

My Love

You're the air that I breathe
You're the love of my life.
You're everything that I need
I'm so glad to be your wife.

You're the man that I married.
You're the man that I love.
I know we were brought together
by the Man up above.

You mean more to me today
then you will ever know.
I love you ever so much
I just wanted to tell you so.

My Moment In Time

We all need that one special moment.
When we wish that time would stand still.
In which something happened to you
that gave you such a thrill.

Was yours when you first fell in love
or the day that you said I Do?
What was that special moment
that happened to you?

What about the day
When you first became a Mom or Dad,
That should be close to the top
for one of the best days you ever had.

All those moments I've had
and yet another one too,
It is something that I did
That I never thought I would do.

I'm so scared of heights
but I went skydiving with my son.
It was an adventure of a lifetime
and one I'm so glad that I have done.

The excitement that you feel
when you are so high up in the sky.
Makes you forget that if things go wrong
you could literally die.

The time had come
for them to open the door,
It was time to jump
we had to wait no more.

My heart was pounding
and beating so fast.
All these feelings that I was having
I wanted them to last.

I'll never forget this special moment
that I shared with my son,
it was one of the best times of my life
and it was so much fun.

What will be my next moment in time
I don't know it yet,
But I do know that it will be
one that I will never forget.

Reflection In The Mirror

As I walked down the hall
I glanced to the right.
What I saw in the mirror
gave me such a fright.

Who was that woman
staring back at me?
I looked again
and wondered how this could be?

I kept staring at the woman
even though I knew it was impolite.
I wanted a better look
so I turned on the light.

This couldn't be me
was all I could say,
What happened to me
in just one day?

The woman in the mirror
had broken teeth and gray hair.
My hair is brown
and my teeth are all there.

How was this possible
I just couldn't figure this out.
I had to know
without a single doubt.

Suddenly I woke up
and knew what this had to be.
I had been dreaming
that the woman I saw was me.

I went straight for the mirror
I had to look and see.
If my own reflection was there
just like it should be.

As I looked in the mirror
I knew one day I would see.
An old woman with gray hair and no teeth
and it would be me.

My Son, David

I'm sitting here looking at you
And wondering where the time has gone
You're a grown man now
My how the time has flown

It was the most perfect October day
When I gave birth to you
You were so beautiful and precious
You made all my dreams come true

I couldn't believe I was a Mother
And this gift from God was my son
When you opened your eyes and looked at me
Without even trying my heart you had won

What a beautiful baby you were
And ever so sweet too
But before I knew it
You were ready to go to school

How many times you use to tell me
Mom I'm getting as tall as you
And I knew it wouldn't be long
Before that was really true

I can't look you squarely in the eyes anymore
Unless you bend down to me
You keep telling me I'm getting shorter
But you keep getting taller you see

You seem to stand as tall
As a mighty oak tree
You can look kind of mean
But you are as sweet as can be

You have a very caring spirit
And such a great big wonderful heart
You never cease to amaze me
With the way you are so smart.

Anytime that I need you
I turn around and there you stand
Not my little boy anymore
But a very handsome young man

David, you've turned out to be
A gentleman in every way
Your father and I are so proud of you
And we thank God for you everyday

The bond between a mother and her son
Is one that will last her whole life thru
I know that my life has been blessed David
By having a son like you

My Valentine

A beautiful cold Sunday afternoon
we said I do.
It was on Valentine's day
that I married you.

As I walked down the aisle
and saw your face.
I knew no one else
could ever take your place.

You looked so handsome
waiting there for me.
I knew by your side
I was meant to be.

As we said our vows
and became man and wife,
I knew I had found my soul mate
for the rest of my life.

32 years have gone by
and my love continues to grow.
I love you more today than then
and just wanted you to know.

My Youngest Son, My Hero

Bobby was only eighteen
when he joined the Corps.
He wanted to serve his country
and fight in the war.

I remember that horrible day
when the call came.
It was time for him to go
they had called his name.

They issued him a gun
and told him to go fight.
It torn my heart out to see him go
but I watched until he was out of sight.

Off to Iraq he was sent
a young man with his gun.
To fight for what he believed
until this war was won.

We will never know
the things he saw or had to do.
He was there to preserve our freedom
and to protect the red white and blue.

Yes this is my hero
my youngest son.
Who was sent off to war
to fight with a gun.

He gave up his youth
to fight in this war.
Hoping that one day
there would be no more.

No Work Today

It's much too pretty outside
To go into work today.
But I have to come up with a reason
So at home I can stay.

I could say my husband is sick
And the kids are too!
Oh wait, I'm not married
So that won't do.

I could say I have to stay with my Mom
Because she has the flu,
No, that won't work either
She lives in Timbuktu.

I could just tell them the truth
And say I just don't want to come in.
Yeah that would go over great
I'd never have to worry about this job again.

Okay so I will just get dressed
And off to work I will go.
Then maybe after an hour or two
I could get sick you know.

I pull into the parking lot
But no cars do I see,
Did they cancel work
And no one told me?

Someone should be here
But where are they?
Oh no, I remember now
I didn't have to come into work – it's Saturday!

Opening The Door

I stand outside the door
afraid to go in.
Did I just hear a sound
or perhaps just the wind.

Dare I knock?
If so what shall I see?
I realized I did not know
how all this came to be.

How did I get here?
Where does the door go to?
Do I just walk on by
or dare I go thru?

I take the knob
afraid to let it go
Do I turn it
I truly just don't know.

My heart is pounding
I know what I must do.
My hands are shaking
as I open the door and go through.

What I will find
I truly do not know.
But thru this door
I know I must go.

Orange Construction Barrels

Orange construction barrels and I
have a problem you see,
on what part of the road belongs to them
and what part belongs to me.

Not long ago I stopped at a red light,
and I turned out to be first in line.
I knew right then I was in trouble
because there were so many cars behind.

The light turned green
and my yellow bug led the way.
It wasn't long before I realized
That we had gone astray.

I started hitting big holes
and knew something was wrong.
As the road got worse,
I knew then I was not where I belonged.

As I looked all around
not a single car was behind me.
It was just me in my yellow bug
on a road that we shouldn't be.

I looked in my rear view mirror
and a construction man I did see.
He was laughing so hard
and it was all because of me.

I was in the middle of the construction
and I knew without a single doubt.
I was going to find it hard
to ever find my way back out.

I looked for some type of exit.
But the only thing I could see,
was now the construction man
was bent over double laughing at me.

The road was so bad now
I knew I was in the worse part.
I made up my mind to find my way out
and from this construction area depart.

There up ahead was a very small path
that would take me back to the light.
It would get me out of this construction area
and this terrible plight.

I quickly turned and got on that path
and back to the highway I did go.
I never once looked back
but this one thing I do know.

I'm sure the road construction man
has told everyone about the way.
How a woman in a yellow vw beetle
gave him such a laugh that day.

Paths?

If we took what we learned
from our past mistakes,
and used that wisdom today
would more we make?

Or would we try
to do the right thing,
and see all the goodness
that this would bring.

We are given choices
and it is up to us to choose,
which one do we pick
to win or to lose?

The paths we choose
and which way we go,
is only for one person
to really know.

But we are only human
and mistakes we are going to do.
How we deal with them
is up to me and you.

We should look back
at the ones we did before
and learn from those
and not make anymore.

Peace of Mind

I've looked high and low
and I can't find,
what happened to
my peace of mind.

I've looked inside
and outside too.
Now what in the world
am I going to do?

I had it yesterday
or was it the day before?
Oh it's starting to happen
I can't remember things anymore.

If you happen to find it
Or know where it might be.
Won't you pick up the phone
and call me.

I'll be so happy
to have it back,
Then my peace of mind
no longer will I lack.

Perfect World

If we were all perfect
then we would all be the same.
We would be known as a number
and not by our name.

But we are not perfect
and sometimes life will throw a curve.
You can either stand up and face it
or try to avoid it with a swerve.

When problems come your way
as they so often do.
You need to rely on your faith
and God will show you what to do.

Life is not easy
and sometimes not even fair.
We all have problems to face
but do we dare?

Do we step up to the bat
and face it head on?
Or do we just ignore it
and try to leave it alone.

Problems have to be solved.
they don't just go away.
You might forget about them for a while
but they are still there every day.

There is no rhyme or reason
for the things we go thru,
It's just the way life is
for me and you.

She Keeps Waiting

The delicate rose you gave to me
I clutch so tightly in my hand.
I keep watching and waiting for you
but you are not here and I don't understand.

You pledged your love to me
as I did mine to you.
You said we would be together always
but now what am I to do?

The night is getting darker
and so much colder too.
It's snowing much heavier now
as I stand here still waiting for you.

My once beautiful rose has now wilted.
The petals are falling one by one.
I try to put them back on
but I can't undo the damage that is done.

I keep staring at the same place.
I'm so afraid to look away.
I'm scared that you won't see me
when you come back this way.

I keep waiting and watching
but how much longer do I stay?
Something must have happened
that has kept you away.

But no matter how long it takes
you'll find me here waiting for you,
Because I know in my heart.
this is what I must do.

Slowly Losing You

We have been thru a lot
in our years together.
Our love grew stronger
even during the stormy weather.

But I have hurt you
and the damage has been done.
And no matter what I do
this battle cannot be won.

You try to remain the same
but you are different now.
I wish I could undo the damage
but I just don't know how.

I don't feel the closeness
that we once knew.
All I really want
is what I use to have with you.

I see the pain in your eyes
even though you think I don't see.
It hurts me to know
it is there because of me.

I know you don't understand
but neither do I.
All I ask of you
is to please try.

I don't want to give up
and let you go.
You mean the world to me
and I love you so.

One day I hope you will forgive me
for the wrong that I have done.
But until that day I will fight for you
until this battle I have won.

So Little Happiness

As I look around the world today
so much sadness do I see.
What has happened to make it that way
how did this come to be?

Why can't we all be happy
we should all be so glad.
Be satisfied with what we have
and not be so sad

We don't take the time
to really enjoy each day.
We just get thru it
each in our own special way.

We rush and rush
and whatever for.
Just to get up the next morning
to do the same thing once more.

There has to be more in life
than taxes and death.
Let's all take a minute to stop
and catch our breath.

We have no guarantees
that tomorrow will come.
We must start to change our ways
before this day is done.

All of us have so much
to be so thankful for
But it is just in our nature
to always want more.

You may not realize this
but just stop and look around you.
You touch so many people everyday
in everything that you do.

We cannot change the world overnight
but we can make a difference you see.
It will take all of us making an effort
and not just you and me.

So today let's try something different
as you go and start your day.
Put a big smile upon your face
and give it to others along your way.

You can't help but smile back
when you see someone smiling at you.
So Smile at everyone you meet
and not just at one or two.

If they in turn will do the same
maybe a difference we will finally see.
That people will no longer be so sad
and they will continue smiling and be Happy.

So Young

He was not expecting
the news that he just heard.
He tried to think back
and remember each word.

Was there any hope
did the doctor say?
They would try and fight it
in every possible way.

He could not think straight
he had to clear his head.
He would have to tell his family
and that is what he dread.

How would they take it
should he just lie?
Did he really have to tell them
that he was going to die?

Cancer was what the doctor said
that was taking his life.
How could he tell his kids
and especially his wife?

Things like this are not suppose to happen
to someone as young as he.
He thought he would live for quite a while
and not die at thirty three.

When the doctor mentioned cancer
and that it was wide spread,
he could not remember after that
what all the doctor said.

His mind was racing
on where he needed to start.
He found the answer
once he stopped and listened to his heart.

He got down on his knees
and prayed to the man above.
Please give him the strength and words
to tell those that he loved.

He knew with God's help
that somehow he would get thru.
And God would show him
exactly what he needed to do.

Prayers were the answer
that could change the outcome.
He wasn't about to give up
with living - he wasn't done.

He got up from his knees
with a different outlook.
And the fears that he once felt
from his body he shook.

It wasn't his time
he knew that in his heart.
He was going to live
and not from his loved ones depart.

With his faith renewed
he would get on with his life.
Now he knew what to tell his kids
and his wife.

Soul Searching

I took a journey today
Into the very depths of my soul
I wanted to find out more about me
So inward I had to go

When I took the first step
It seemed like I fell forever
Then I slowed down
Wanting to learn from this endeavor

I didn't know what to expect
Or the things that I would see
But I felt very calm
Seeing these things about me

I saw confusion and anxiety
And the stress that it caused me
I saw love and compassion
With its peace and serenity

So many things I was seeing
That it was hard to comprehend
I wanted to learn more
So I continued to descend

It started getting darker
But a light I did see
It seemed as though
It was beckoning to me

I wanted to go toward it
But try as I might
I couldn't get any closer
To this blinding light

Before I was ready
For this adventure to end
I found myself
Coming out from within

I felt kind of different
From this trip that I took
I wanted to see if there were changes
So in the mirror I did look

I still looked the same
But a little difference I could see
That face in the mirror
Looking back was still me!

Super Mom

My home was once a house
but not anymore.
It is now a warm comfortable home
that I truly adore.

I used to work myself to death
trying to get it all done.
But that battle is finally over
because I never won.

There was always dinner to cook
and lessons to do.
Oh yes let's not forget the laundry
although I tried too.

The weekends would come
but they would go so fast.
No matter what I did
daylight just wouldn't last.

There were groceries to buy
and a house to clean.
I tried to do it all
you know what I mean?

I tried to be a Super Mom
but there was no way.
I never got to enjoy
any part of my day.

But that is what I always wanted
to be a Mother and wife,
To have those I had to give up
what was once my life.

I know that if I could
do it all over again.
I would do it in a heartbeat
and this time that battle I would win!

The Door Of Opportunities

When looking at your life
Are you happy with what you see?
Or are you just content
With what you turned out to be?

The opportunities are unlimited
And far beyond compare.
Are you willing to do what it takes
To get you there?

Sometimes you have to take a chance
And open up a door.
All the wonders of the world
Wait for you there and even more.

Will you be one that takes a chance
And see what the world offers you?
Or will you just stand at the door in fear
And not know what to do?

Life doesn't come with instructions
So there will be choices we will have to make.
Are you ready to face the consequences
In case you make a mistake?

Don't be one that waits too long
Step up and see what waits for you.
Turn the handle on the door
And step right on thru.

The Joys Of Being A Mother

You hear a cry
and you start to cry too.
The doctor has just handed
your baby boy to you.

You have become a Mother
something that you always wanted to be.
At least that is how it was
when it happened to me.

When I held my son in my arms
for the very first time,
I couldn't believe this little miracle
this little boy was all mine.

I touched his tiny little face
and just held him in my arms.
I wanted to protect him
and keep him from all harm.

I never knew my heart
could hold so much love and joy,
as I was experiencing
just from holding my little boy.

Several years have now passed
and my boys became young men.
Ah to go back to those early days
when they were little again.

But no matter
how old or big they become.
To me they will always be
my little boys - My sons.

David and Bobby
I just want the two of you to know
that you have given me so much love and joy
and I dearly love you both so.

Just know too that no matter
Where you go or what you do
Your Mother's love will always be
Right there with you.

The Letter

I'm writing you this letter
to say goodbye to you.
It's time I closed this chapter
and finally realize we are thru.

I've held on to your memories
and what I thought could be,
The most wonderful life
between you and me.

It was over years ago
but still I held on,
To what I thought could have been
even though we found new loves of our own.

I hope life has been good to you
as it has been for me,
I know now the love I have
Is the one that was truly meant to be.

This letter I will never mail
Nor these words will you see,
It's just my way to say goodbye to you
and to the love that could never be.

The Man On The Corner

He was standing on the street corner
with an old metal can clutched in his hand.
His clothes all ragged and dirty
you could barely make out he was a man.

He looked so frail and ever so thin.
Just looking at him, my heart ached so.
It was all I could do just to stand there
because I really wanted to turn and go.

But something about him made me stay
so I kept watching him from afar.
He was so oblivious to what was going on
that he was almost hit by a car.

I slowly walked up to where he stood
and reached out to take his hand.
I saw a tear slowly run down his face
as I gently dropped some money in his can.

He told me his name was John,
and that he had been living out on the streets.
With the money he had made today
he was going to go get something to eat.

I took him to a place right down the way
I wanted to make sure that he ate.
We ordered him several things from the menu
and he ate everything on his plate.

We sat there for a while
and John just seemed to open up to me.
He told me how in one week he lost his job
and then his wife and family.

He said that he had nowhere to go
and he had no place to stay.
That's how he ended upon the streets
Where he is today.

He couldn't thank me enough
for everything that I had done.
A special place in his heart
he said that I had won.

I watched him get up from the table
then very quietly go out the door.
I knew once that he had left
that I would see him no more.

Several days thereafter
I went by his corner hoping that I would see
him standing there with his old metal can
but it just wasn't meant to be.

I found out that John had died
his cancer was too far progressed.
I know that John is now in Heaven
where he is finally able to rest.

The Road Of Life

The road of life
is full of choices that we must make.
Whether good or bad
the consequences we must take.

I wish that road
only ran one way.
And there would be no obstacles
that would lead us astray.

How simple life would be
if everything went right.
Our worries would be none
and our burdens would be light.

But bad decisions do happen
and we must face up to them.
Whether here on earth
or in front of Him.

But what if God gave us the power
to go back and undo
something in our life?
Would I take that chance - would you?

Correcting one thing
might lead to making more.
Only God knows
what life holds in store.

It would be hard to choose
even if we tried with all our might.
What we would change
in our life to make it right.

Sometimes things don't turn out
the way that we wish they would.
But having the bad things come along
makes us appreciate more the good.

So when you make choices in your life,
Make sure it's the right one.
I know this to be true
You can't go back and get it undone

Then And Now

I think there is someone
in everyone's past,
that you never forget
even though it didn't last.

You fell in love
and gave them your heart.
Never thinking that one day
you would eventually part.

That wonderful feeling
still comes to mind.
The one you thought
was one of a kind.

But what if you could
go back in time?
And you look at these things
now with an open mind.

You could now see
things weren't right.
Even though you tried
with all your might.

It wasn't meant to be
so we went separate ways.
But you still catch yourself
looking back to those days.

But then you realize
something better came along.
And it was the real thing
you're right where you belong.

This Man Of Mine

I don't know where to begin
or even where to start.
To tell you about this man
that literally stole my heart.

He's everything I ever wanted
or ever hoped to find.
He's the answer to all my dreams
this wonderful man of mine.

He shows his love to me
in so many different ways.
He doesn't even have to tell me
but he does each and every day.

God has truly blessed me
by giving me this man.
I will do my best to keep him happy
by doing everything that I can.

I don't know how I got so lucky
but I know this much is true,
I love this man with all my heart
and he loves me that much too!

This Man That I Love

He doesn't know that I'm looking at him
while he is sitting over there.
He's watching one of his tv shows
all leaned back in his favorite chair.

This is the man I married
so many years ago.
I never knew that someone
could love me so.

I reach out to touch his hand
and he turns to look at me.
He smiles and tells me he loves me
and I'm as content as can be.

I see the love in his eyes
and I know it's there for me.
I never knew life could be so good
and that I could so happy.

I love this man so much.
He is the love of my life.
I thank God every day for bringing us together
and for making me his wife.

We will always be together.
He and I.
I will love him forever
and even after I die!

To Have Loved And Lost

If you could make a choice
before this happened to you?
I've often wondered
what people would actually do?

Is it better to have loved and lost
than never to have loved at all?
Is it better to experience that feeling
then turn around and lose it all?

I wish life came with answers
in telling us what we should do.
But that is not the way God intended
for it to be for me and you.

So my answer on what I would do
about better to have loved and lost.
Would be yes without a doubt
even at the cost.

I knew that kind of love once before
but it wasn't meant to be.
That was not the true love
that God wanted for me.

My heart knew what love actually was
and I knew I wanted that feeling again.
So I took another chance
and I'm so glad because this time I did win!

God gave me a second chance
and sent me my one true love.
He turned out to be my soul mate
who was sent from heaven above.

So take that chance at love
No matter what you do,
There is someone out there waiting
And they are waiting - just for you!

To Mother With Love

I don't have to rush out and buy a gift
or even go get a card.
When Mother's day comes each year
it is always so hard.

It's been five years
since you have been gone.
But there are days
that it doesn't seem that long.

I miss your smiling face
and hearing your laughter too.
Oh how I wish that I could
just sit and talk with you.

I miss your voice
just saying my name.
Days without you being here
just aren't the same.

You were the most
loving and caring person I knew.
There was nothing for anybody
that you wouldn't do.

A part of you will always live on
in each of our hearts and mind.
You taught us how to love
and to be gentle and kind.

These traits we will pass on
to each of our kids too.
So that your memory will continue
and we will never forget you.

I go and visit your grave site
and sit quietly and talk to you.
I tell you all the things
that has happened and what I'm going thru.

I wait patiently to hear your reply
and you telling me what I should do.
But no sounds do I hear.
Oh Mother how I miss you!

You were such a very special person
that loved and was very loved.
But we knew it was your time and you had to go
to be with Jesus in your home up above.

Just know on this Mother's Day
and everyday throughout the year,
your children miss you so much
but in our hearts you'll always be near.

To Thine Own Self Be True

Tiny little secrets
that you tell no one.
You think will not hurt
oh but the damage that is done.

The secrets will eat at you
like some sort of disease.
You can't sleep or eat
yourself you cannot please.

You should have told him
right from the start.
Now you wonder
is there still love in his heart?

When he finds out
the secrets that you had.
You'll see it in his eyes
that he is so sad.

You have hurt him so much
but you hurt yourself to.
Remember the old saying
to thine own self be true.

You look at yourself in the mirror
at the person you have become.
You are torn in so many directions
but this battle cannot be won

You look again at yourself
and see what you must do
You can't go on
until you forgive You.

Once you do that
You go to your loved one
And hopefully things will work out
Because the right thing you have done

Trudy, My Little Sister

I want to tell you about someone
and she just happens to be,
someone I dearly love
she's my little sister, Trudy.

She has been there for me
in the good times and bad.
She laughs with me when I'm happy
and cries with me when I'm sad.

The two of us are very close
though we are several years apart.
I have a very special place just for her
deep inside my heart.

We do have a lot of fun
when we are around each other.
I remember when she was very little
she called me her second Mother.

Sometimes she likes to be in control
because that is just her way.
So she will tell us what we have to do
and we better listen to what she has to say.

She's all grown now
married and with kids of her own.
She lives far away in another city
nowhere close to my home.

We don't call as often
each other as we use to.
Sometimes we will just send a text
and that is so bad for us to do.

But if one of us needs the other one,
we will always be right there.
It's all for one and one for all
because we do truly care.

Trudy I just want you to know
you are more than just my sister - you are my best Friend,
and if and when you ever need me
I'll be there for you until the very end.

I Love You!

T'was The Day Before Christmas

T'was the day before Christmas
and not a sound do I hear.
The silence was deafening
upon my ears.

No arguments no fighting
are these kids really mine?
And to one another
they were actually being kind.

Please and thank you
were things that I heard.
Other than that
they never uttered a word.

This was too good to be true
I just couldn't figure it out.
Then it dawned on me
what this was all about.

They had to be good
they had been warned.
They promised to be on their best behavior
to Santa they had sworn.

Santa was coming
in fact that very night.
That is why the kids were so good
and that was quite alright.

I knew I had better enjoy this
because it wasn't going to last.
Santa was already making his rounds
and he was coming fast.

So off to bed
they all did go,
The sooner they went to sleep
the sooner Santa would show.

Later I too headed up the stairs
and as I did turned off the lights.
I took one last look back down
and saw to my delight.

The presents placed where the kids could see
next day in the early morning light.
So only one thing left to do and say
Merry Christmas to all and to all a Good Night.

Welcome to Motherhood

Something inside of you just moved
and how weird it was to feel.
You realize this is not a dream
this is something very real.

For nine months
your child was inside of you.
But now they want out
oh, Lord what shall I do!

Now your baby has arrived
and the doctor gives it to you.
But where's the instructions
that tell me what to do?

Your day starts at 2:00 am
and then you're back up again at 4
You change his diaper and feed him
but in two hours he'll just want more!

He's had a full day
and so have you.
But tomorrow it starts all over
at least you're learning what to do.

As you lay him down
you take another look.
You've made it one whole day
without an instruction book!

You did everything
just like you should.
You have now made it
into Motherhood.

The pay is pretty lousy
but the benefits are like no other,
Your name has changed also
you are now officially – a Mother!

What If

What if God gave you
the insight to see.
The upcoming things
that would happen to you and me.

You could not interfere
with the things you saw.
They were only yours to observe
and that was all.

Would you be scared?
Would you still want to see?
These things that would be happening
to you and to me.

You couldn't even alter anything
happening to the ones you dearly love.
Especially if it was their time
to join the man above.

But what if one of the things you could see
was the day you would die.
Still there would be nothing that you could do
no matter how hard you try.

Would this make you change anything
about how you live each day?
Or would you continue
doing what you do in the same way?

We all think that we have plenty of time
to set our lives straight.
But our future is not certain
So please don't wait.

To know the love of Jesus
and to be saved by his grace,
you will know when you leave this earth
that you've gone to a much better place.

So no what ifs will be happening
for God is the only one to see.
These things that will happen and when
to you and to me.

Who's Your Favorite

I'm sure this happens in every family.
Kids wanting to know
who is your favorite child
so they can say see I told you so!

There was five of us kids growing up
and needless to say
we drove my Mom crazy
asking her this each and every day.

Mom I know I'm your favorite
but we won't tell the others.
I know you love me more
than my sisters and my brothers.

Even my two boys
Ask this of me almost every day.
They truly think one of them is my favorite
no matter what I say.

So the next time
one of your kids ask you.
Mom who's your favorite
here's what you can do.

Join in the game
and have a little fun with it too.
Tell them the other child is your favorite
And just see what they do!

Why Lord?

Lord, my shoulders are heavy
from the burdens that I bare.
But I know I don't have to carry them alone
because you are always there .

We all have moments
when things just get out of hand.
But Lord tell me why it has to be this way
so that I will better understand.

I know that no matter what we do
where we go, or what we say.
You are always there for us
and you will never go away.

So why can't we do that
and never turn our backs on you.
The world would be a much better place
if that is what we would learn to do.

There is so much hatred
In the world today
Help me Lord to know the reason
Why it has to be that way

Why are people killing other people
Try as I might I still don't understand
Aren't we supposed to be there to help
And not hurt our fellow man

Help me Lord in my everyday life
To always be there the way you are for me
And above all help us to get the world
Back to the way that it used to be

Will You Remember?

I'm no one special
nor do I claim to be.
But I wonder sometimes
will people remember me?

People see me every day
but will they notice if I'm not there?
Will they ever think of me?
Will they even care?

I have friends
some very special to me.
But after a while even to them,
will my memory cease to be?

Time has a way
of helping people deal,
when they lose someone
and the pain that they feel.

When I'm gone
and no longer on this earth.
I want to leave behind
something of worth.

Something that will stand out
that people will see.
And then they will smile
and maybe think of me.

Some people make a difference
and that is what I want to do.
I want to make the world a better place
for each and every one of you.

I want to do something
so people won't forget.
I was once here
and maybe someone they had met.

Maybe one day
before I go,
there will be something I can do
and then people will know.

That I was here
but from this earth I did depart.
My only hope is that a part of me
will forever remain in their hearts.

Winter Time

The clouds are darkening
The wind is starting to get bolder
There is a crispness in the air now
As the weather is starting to get colder

Wintertime is on its way
It has stood idle for so long
Now it is time to make its entrance
And it is coming on strong

The shadows are growing more distant
As the sun fights to stay up high
But the moon is trying to take over
As the two fight up in the sky

People are pulling their coats up close
As the wind whips thru the air
The coldness colors their cheeks
And plays havoc with their hair

The snow is starting to fall
Wintertime has officially begun
Oh how I long for those warm summer days
And sitting out in the sun

If only we could take refuge
And for 3 months just hide away
And only come out again
When the sun will be here to stay

But unfortunately that is not to be
Facing the cold is what we must do
For if you are like me
We each have a job to go to

So to endure these change of seasons
Is something that we must all do
Because that is the way God intended
For it to be for me and you.

You Are Truly My Blessing

The way you smile
when you look at me,
The look of love in your eyes
that only I can see.

When you say my name
and it lingers in the air.
The way you run your fingers
thru my hair.

When you take my hand
and hold it to your cheek,
I know you love me
without having to speak.

It's the little things
that you do,
That make me so happy
and glad that I have you.

You have been a blessing to me
right from the start.
And I'm so grateful that you love me
with all of your heart.

You Touched It

I bet you don't hear this
around your house like I do.
When something goes wrong
do they ever say, it was you?

My confidence level
is not what it used to be.
When something breaks,
my family looks directly at me.

When things quit working
the first thing they say,
mom did you touch it,
and then go on their way.

It makes me wonder why
what's wrong with me.
All I do is touch something.
Then it doesn't work you see.

I turn on the TV
and nothing comes on.
I pick up the phone to call someone,
and something is wrong with the phone.

Why are these things happening,
when I touch them in some sort of way.
After they seem to tear up
I know what my family is going to say.

Mom you touched it!
We told you not to.
Why can't you leave things alone?
Like we told you to do.

One day I won't be around
Then who will they blame,
when things tear up
and don't work the same.

Until that day comes
guess I will continue to be,
the one who always tears things up
because the last one to touch it was me.

About the Author

Jackie Calahan Houk was born and raised in a small town called Shelbyville, Tennessee. Shelbyville is known as the "Pencil City" and the Walking Horse Capital of the World. While she lived in Shelbyville, Jackie worked as a receptionist and secretary at a couple of the pencil companies. When she worked at National Pen and Pencil, she met the man that would steal her heart. His name was George Houk and he was the Plant Engineer there. They got married in 1982 and moved to Murfreesboro, Tennessee were they still reside today.

After they had lived in Murfreesboro for a couple of years, Jackie started to work for State Farm Insurance Company as a Data Entry Clerk. She is now a Human Resource Assistant and has been at State Farm for over 28 years.

Jackie has been writing poems for quite some time. Several years ago she realized how much she enjoyed writing poetry in rhymes. That is when the name of this book developed, Rhymes With A Reason. With the love and encouragement of her family and friends, Jackie decided she would take it more seriously and maybe one day have a book of her poems published.

Jackie and her husband, George, have been happily married for 35 years. George is retired and tells everyone that he can live off of "love" as long as love keeps on working and that is what Jackie does. They have two sons, David and Bobby – who have brought nothing but joy and love into their lives. Even though both of their sons now work for State Farm Insurance, they had both pursued other opportunities earlier in their lives.

David graduated culinary school at Cordon Bleu in Las Vegas and has been a chef at several of the major restaurants throughout Tennessee and Mississippi. Bobby joined the Marines right out of high school at the early age of 18. He served in the Iraq war as a machine gunner in a humvee when he was only 19 years old.

George, David and Bobby have been the inspiration for many of Jackie's poems. Most of her poems are true, however there are a very few that are fiction. As you read them, you will see that even though her poems are simple in verse, they all come directly from her heart.

Jackie has always enjoyed reading poetry and now she hopes that you will enjoy reading hers.